Step-by-Step, Practical Recipes Sweet Treats: Contents

Pies & Tarts

Not only do they look impressive, pies and tarts also make a delicious and versatile treat; from chocolate or nut to fruit or custard, there are so many great flavours to try.

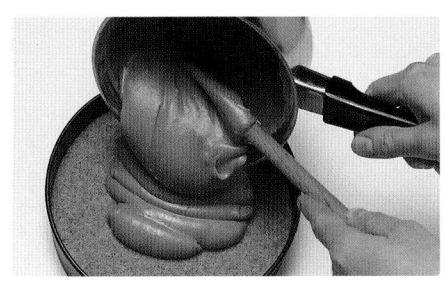

Puddings

From traditional to exotic, there's a pudding to suit everyone. These recipes boast mouthwatering flavours bound to be a hit at family meals or dinner parties.

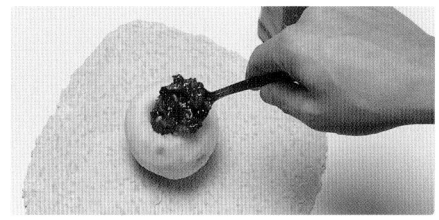

FLAME TREE has been creating family-friendly, classic and beginner recipes for our bestselling cookbooks for over 20 years now. Our mission is to offer you a wide range of expert-tested dishes, while providing clear images of the final dish so that you can match it to your own results. We hope you enjoy this super selection of recipes – there are plenty more to try! Titles in this series include:

**Cupcakes • Slow Cooker • Curries
Soups & Starters • Baking & Breads
Cooking on a Budget • Winter Warmers
Party Cakes • Meat Eats • Party Food
Chocolate • Sweet Treats**

www.flametreepublishing.com

Chocolate Mallow Pie

INGREDIENTS

Serves 6

200 g/7 oz digestive biscuits
75 g/3 oz butter, melted
175 g/6 oz plain dark chocolate
20 marshmallows
1 medium egg, separated
300 ml/¹⁄₂ pint double cream

1 Place the biscuits in a polythene bag and finely crush with a rolling pin. Alternatively, place in a food processor and blend until fine crumbs are formed.

2 Melt the butter in a medium-sized sauce-pan, add the crushed biscuits and mix together. Press into the base of the prepared tin and leave to cool in the refrigerator.

3 Melt 125 g/4 oz of the chocolate with the marshmallows and 2 tablespoons of water in a saucepan over a gentle heat, stirring constantly. Leave to cool slightly, then stir in the egg yolk, beat well, then return to the refrigerator until cool.

4 Whisk the egg white until stiff and standing in peaks, then fold into the chocolate mixture.

5 Lightly whip the cream and fold three-quarters of the cream into the chocolate mixture. Reserve the remainder. Spoon the chocolate cream into the flan case and chill in the refrigerator until set.

6 When ready to serve, spoon the remaining cream over the chocolate pie, swirling in a decorative pattern. Grate the remaining dark chocolate and sprinkle over the cream, then serve.

TASTY TIP

Replace the digestive biscuits with an equal weight of chocolate-covered digestive biscuits to make a quick change to this recipe.

2

3

5

Lattice Treacle Tart

INGREDIENTS

Serves 4

For the pastry:
175 g/6 oz plain flour
40 g/1½ oz butter
40 g/1½ oz white vegetable fat

For the filling:
225 g/8 oz golden syrup
finely grated rind and juice
 of 1 lemon
75 g/3 oz fresh white breadcrumbs
1 small egg, beaten

1 Preheat the oven to 190°C/375°F/Gas Mark 5. Make the pastry by placing the flour, butter and white vegetable fat in a food processor. Blend in short sharp bursts until the mixture resembles fine breadcrumbs. Remove from the processor and place on a pastry board or in a large bowl.

2 Stir in enough cold water to make a dough and knead in a large bowl or on a floured surface until smooth and pliable.

3 Roll out the pastry and use to line a 20.5 cm/ 8 inch loose-bottomed fluted flan dish or tin. Reserve the pastry trimmings for decoration. Chill for 30 minutes.

4 Meanwhile, to make the filling, place the golden syrup in a saucepan and warm gently with the lemon rind and juice. Tip the breadcrumbs into the pastry case and pour the syrup mixture over the top.

5 Roll the pastry trimmings out on a lightly floured surface and cut into 6–8 thin strips. Lightly dampen the pastry edge of the tart, then place the strips across the filling in a lattice pattern. Brush the ends of the strips with water and seal to the edge of the tart. Brush a little beaten egg over the pastry and bake in the preheated oven for a 25 minutes, or until the filling is just set. Serve hot or cold.

TASTY TIP
Why not replace the breadcrumbs with the same amount of desiccated coconut?

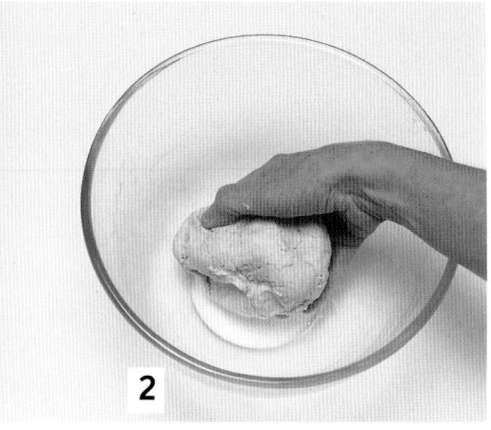

2

4

5

Double Chocolate Banoffee Tart

INGREDIENTS

Cuts into 8 slices

2 x 400 g cans sweetened
  condensed milk
175 g/6 oz plain dark
  chocolate, chopped
600 ml/1 pint whipping cream
1 tbsp golden syrup
25 g/1 oz butter, diced
150 g/5 oz white chocolate, grated
  or finely chopped
1 tsp vanilla essence
2–3 ripe bananas
cocoa powder, for dusting

For the ginger crumb crust:

24–26 gingernut biscuits,
  roughly crushed
100 g/3½ oz butter, melted
½ tbsp sugar, or to taste
½ tsp ground ginger

TASTY TIP

Do not assemble the tart more than 2–3 hours before serving as it will go too soft.

1 Preheat the oven to 190°C/375°F/Gas Mark 5, 10 minutes before baking. Place the condensed milk in a heavy-based saucepan and place over a gentle heat. Bring to the boil, stirring constantly. Boil gently for about 3–5 minutes or until golden. Remove from the heat and leave to cool.

2 To make the crust, place the biscuits with the melted butter, sugar and ginger in a food processor and blend together. Press into the sides and base of 23 cm/9 inch loose-based flan tin with the back of a spoon. Chill in the refrigerator for 15–20 minutes, then bake in the preheated oven for 5–6 minutes. Remove from the oven and leave to cool.

3 Melt the dark chocolate in a medium-sized saucepan with 150 ml/ ¼ pint of the whipping cream, the golden syrup and the butter over a low heat. Stir until smooth. Carefully pour into the crumb crust, tilting the tin to distribute the chocolate layer evenly. Chill in the refrigerator for at least 1 hour or until set.

4 Heat 150 ml/¼ pint of the remaining cream until hot, then add all the white chocolate and stir until melted and smooth. Stir in the vanilla essence and strain into a bowl. Leave to cool to room temperature.

5 Scrape the cooked condensed milk into a bowl and whisk until smooth, adding a little of the remaining cream if too thick. Spread over the chocolate layer, then slice the bananas and arrange evenly over the top.

6 Whisk the remaining cream until soft peaks form. Stir a spoonful of the cream into the white chocolate mixture, then fold in the remaining cream. Spread over the bananas, swirling to the edge. Dust with cocoa powder and chill in the refrigerator until ready to serve.

3

5

6

Chocolate Apricot Linzer Torte

INGREDIENTS

Cuts into 10–12 slices

For the chocolate almond pastry:
75 g/3 oz whole blanched almonds
125 g/4 oz caster sugar
215 g/7½ oz plain flour
2 tbsp cocoa powder
1 tsp ground cinnamon
½ tsp salt
grated zest of 1 orange
225 g/8 oz unsalted butter, diced
2–3 tbsp iced water

For the filling:
350 g/12 oz apricot jam
75 g/3 oz milk chocolate, chopped
icing sugar, for dusting

1 Preheat the oven to 375°C/190°F/Gas Mark 5, 10 minutes before baking. Lightly oil a 28 cm/11 inch flan tin. Place the almonds and half the sugar into a food processor and blend until finely ground. Add the remaining sugar, flour, cocoa powder, cinnamon, salt and orange zest and blend again. Add the diced butter and blend in short bursts to form coarse crumbs. Add the water 1 tablespoon at a time until the mixture starts to come together.

2 Turn onto a lightly floured surface and knead lightly, roll out, then using your fingertips, press half the dough onto the base and sides of the tin. Prick the base with a fork and chill in the refrigerator. Roll out the remaining dough between 2 pieces of clingfilm to a 28–30.5 cm/11–12 inch round. Slide the round onto a baking sheet and chill in the refrigerator for 30 minutes.

3 For the filling, spread the apricot jam evenly over the chilled pastry base and sprinkle with the chopped chocolate.

4 Slide the dough round onto a lightly floured surface and peel off the top layer of clingfilm. Using a straight edge, cut the round into 1 cm/½ inch strips; allow to soften until slightly flexible. Place half the strips, about 1 cm/½ inch apart, to create a lattice pattern. Press down on each side of each crossing to accentuate the effect. Press the ends of the strips to the edge, cutting off any excess. Bake in the preheated oven for 35 minutes, or until cooked. Leave to cool before dusting with icing sugar and serve cut into slices.

TASTY TIP
When making the pastry do not allow the dough to form into a ball or it will be tough.

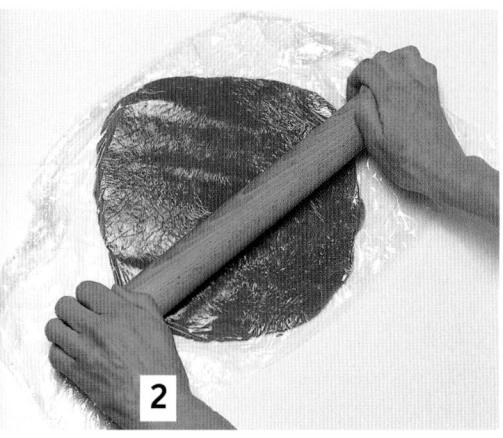

2

3

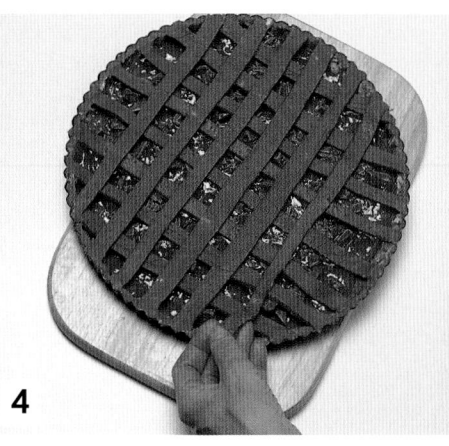

4

Chocolate Peanut Butter Pie

INGREDIENTS

Cuts into 8 slices

22–24 chocolate wafers or peanut
butter cookies
100 g/3½ oz butter, melted
1–2 tbsp sugar
1 tsp vanilla essence
1½ tbsp gelatine
100 g/3½ oz caster sugar
1 tbsp cornflour
½ tsp salt
225 ml/8 fl oz milk
2 large eggs, separated
2 large egg yolks
100 g/3½ oz plain dark
chocolate, chopped
2 tbsp rum or 2 tsp vanilla essence
125 g/4 oz smooth peanut butter
300 ml/½ pint whipping cream
chocolate curls, to decorate

1 Place the wafers or cookies with the melted butter, sugar and vanilla essence in a food processor and blend together. Press into the base of 23 cm/9 inch flat tin. Chill in the refrigerator for 15–20 minutes.

2 Place 3 tablespoons of cold water in a bowl and sprinkle over the powdered gelatine, leave until softened.

3 Blend half the sugar with the cornflour and salt in a heavy-based saucepan and gradually whisk in the milk. Bring to the boil, then reduce the heat and boil gently for 1–2 minutes, or until thickened and smooth, stirring constantly.

4 Beat all the egg yolks together then whisk in half the hot milk mixture and whisk until blended. Whisk in the remaining milk mixture, return to a clean saucepan and cook gently until the mixture comes to the boil and thickens. Boil, stirring vigorously, for 1 minute, then pour a quarter of the custard into a bowl. Add the chopped chocolate and rum or vanilla essence and stir until the chocolate has melted and the mixture is smooth. Pour into the chocolate crust and chill in the refrigerator until set.

5 Whisk the softened gelatine into the remaining custard and whisk until thoroughly dissolved. Whisk in the peanut butter until melted and smooth. Whisk the egg whites until stiff, then whisk in the remaining sugar, 1 tablespoon at a time.

6 Whip the cream until soft peaks form. Fold 125 ml/4 fl oz of the cream into the custard, then fold in the egg whites. Spread the peanut butter cream mixture over the chocolate layer. Spread or pipe over the surface with the remaining cream, forming decorative swirls. Decorate with chocolate curls and chill in the refrigerator until ready to serve.

1

3

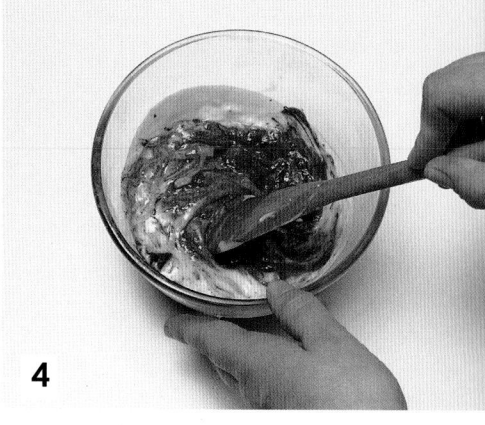
4

White Chocolate & Macadamia Tartlets

INGREDIENTS

Makes 10

300 g/11 oz ready-made sweet
  shortcrust pastry, thawed if frozen
2 medium eggs
50 g/2 oz caster sugar
250 ml/9 fl oz golden syrup
40 g/1½ oz butter, melted
50 ml/2 fl oz whipping cream
1 tsp vanilla or almond essence
225 g/8 oz unsalted macadamia nuts,
  coarsely chopped
150 g/5 oz white chocolate,
  coarsely chopped

1 Preheat the oven to 200°C/ 400°F/Gas Mark 6, 15 minutes before baking. Roll the pastry out on a lightly floured surface and use to line 10 x 7.5–9 cm/3–3½ inch tartlet tins. Line each tin with a small piece of tinfoil and fill with baking beans. Arrange on a baking sheet and bake blind in the preheated oven for 10 minutes. Remove the tinfoil and baking beans and leave to cool.

2 Beat the eggs with the sugar until light and creamy, then beat in the golden syrup, the butter, cream and vanilla or almond essence. Stir in the macadamia nuts. Sprinkle 100 g/3½ oz of the chopped white chocolate equally over the bases of the tartlet cases and divide the mixture evenly among them.

3 Reduce the oven temperature to 180°C/350°F/Gas Mark 4 and bake the tartlets for 20 minutes, or until the tops are puffy and golden and the filling is set. Remove from the oven and leave to cool on a wire rack.

4 Carefully remove the tartlets from their tins and arrange closely together on the wire rack. Melt the remaining white chocolate and, using a teaspoon or a small paper piping bag, drizzle the melted chocolate over the surface of the tartlets in a zig-zag pattern. Serve slightly warm or at room temperature.

FOOD FACT

Macadamia nuts come from Hawaii and are large, crisp, buttery flavoured nuts. They are readily available from supermarkets.

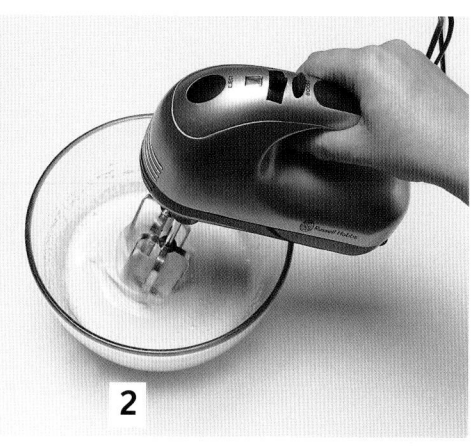

2

2

4

White Chocolate Mousse & Strawberry Tart

INGREDIENTS

Cuts into 10 slices

300 g/11 oz ready-made sweet
   shortcrust pastry, thawed if frozen
60 g/2½ oz strawberry jam
½ tbsp kirsch or framboise liqueur
450–700 g/1–1½ lb ripe strawberries,
   sliced lengthways

For the white chocolate mousse:

250 g/9 oz white chocolate, chopped
350 ml/12 oz double cream
3 tbsp kirsch or framboise liqueur
1–2 large egg whites (optional)

HELPFUL HINT

This recipe contains raw egg whites, which should be eaten with caution by vulnerable groups including the elderly, the young and pregnant women. If you are worried, omit them from the recipe.

1 Preheat the oven to 200°C/400°F/Gas Mark 6, 15 minutes before baking. Roll the prepared pastry out on a lightly floured surface and use to line a 25.5 cm/10 inch flan tin.

2 Line with either tinfoil or nonstick baking parchment and baking beans then bake blind in the preheated oven for 15–20 minutes. Remove the tinfoil or baking parchment and return to the oven for a further 5 minutes.

3 To make the mousse, place the white chocolate with 2 tablespoons of water and 125 ml/4 fl oz of the cream in a saucepan and heat gently, stirring until the chocolate has melted and is smooth. Remove from the heat, stir in the kirsch or framboise liqueur and cool.

4 Whip the remaining cream until soft peaks form. Fold a spoonful of the cream into the cooled white chocolate mixture, then fold in the remaining cream. If using, whisk the egg whites until stiff and gently fold into the white chocolate cream mixture to make a softer, lighter mousse. Chill in the refrigerator for 15–20 minutes.

5 Heat the strawberry jam with the kirsch or framboise liqueur and brush or spread half the mixture onto the pastry base. Leave to cool.

6 Spread the chilled chocolate mousse over the jam and arrange the sliced strawberries in concentric circles over the mousse. If necessary, reheat the strawberry jam and glaze the strawberries lightly.

7 Chill the tart in the refrigerator for about 3–4 hours, or until the chocolate mousse has set. Cut into slices and serve.

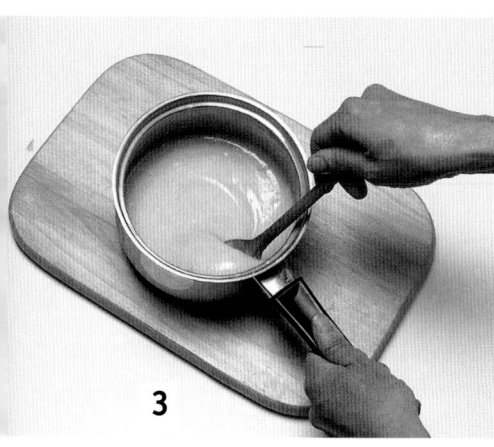

3

4

6

Iced Bakewell Tart

INGREDIENTS

Cuts into 10 slices

For the rich pastry:
175 g/6 oz plain flour
pinch of salt
60 g/2½ oz butter, cut into
   small pieces
50 g/2 oz white vegetable fat,
   cut into small pieces
2 small egg yolks, beaten

For the filling:
125 g/4 oz butter, melted
125 g/4 oz caster sugar
125 g/4 oz ground almonds
2 large eggs, beaten
few drops of almond essence
2 tbsp seedless raspberry jam

For the icing:
125 g/4 oz icing sugar, sifted
6–8 tsp fresh lemon juice
25 g/1 oz toasted flaked almonds

TASTY TIP

It is not essential to use raspberry jam. If there is none in the store cupboard use any seedless jam available. Blackcurrant jam would work particularly well.

1 Preheat the oven to 200°C/400°F/Gas Mark 6. Place the flour and salt in a bowl, rub in the butter and vegetable fat until the mixture resembles breadcrumbs. Alternatively, blend quickly, in short bursts in a food processor.

2 Add the eggs with sufficient water to make a soft, pliable dough. Knead lightly on a floured board then chill in the refrigerator for about 30 minutes. Roll out the pastry and use to line a 23 cm/9 inch loose-bottomed flan tin.

3 For the filling, mix together the melted butter, sugar, almonds and beaten eggs and add a few drops of almond essence. Spread the base of the pastry case with the raspberry jam and spoon over the egg mixture.

4 Bake in the preheated oven for about 30 minutes, or until the filling is firm and golden brown. Remove from the oven and allow to cool completely.

5 When the tart is cold make the icing by mixing together the icing sugar and lemon juice, a little at a time, until the icing is smooth and of a spreadable consistency.

6 Spread the icing over the tart, leave to set for 2–3 minutes and sprinkle with the almonds. Chill in the refrigerator for about 10 minutes and serve.

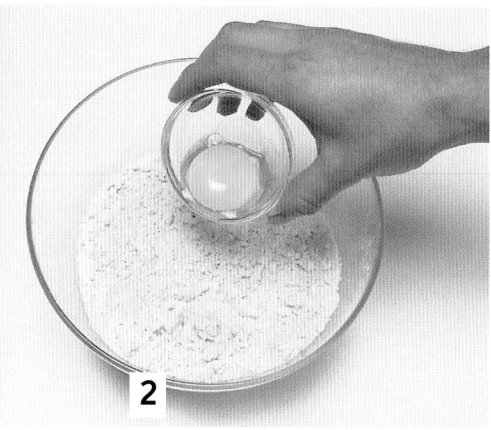

2

3

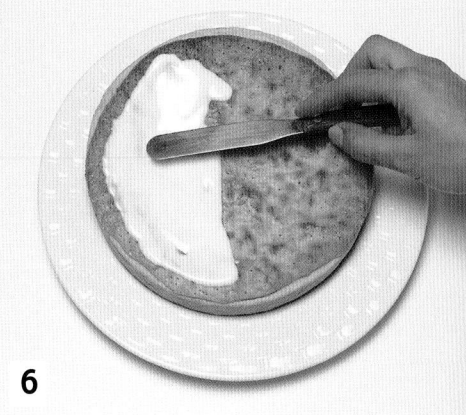

6

Egg Custard Tart

INGREDIENTS

Serves 6

For the sweet pastry:
50 g/2 oz butter
50 g/2 oz white vegetable fat
175 g/6 oz plain flour
1 medium egg yolk, beaten
2 tsp caster sugar

For the filling:
300 ml/½ pint milk
2 medium eggs, plus
  1 medium egg yolk
25 g/1 oz caster sugar
½ tsp freshly grated nutmeg

HELPFUL HINT

Nowadays eggs are normally date stamped so it is possible to ensure that they are eaten when they are at their best. Another way to test if an egg is fresh is to place an uncooked egg in a bowl of water – if it lies at the bottom it is fresh; if it tilts it is older (use for frying or scrambling); if it floats, discard.

1. Preheat the oven to 200°C/400°F/Gas Mark 6. Oil a 20.5 cm/8 inch flan tin or dish.

2. Make the pastry by cutting the butter and vegetable fat into small cubes. Add to the flour in a large bowl and rub in, until the mixture resembles fine breadcrumbs.

3. Add the egg, sugar and enough water to form a soft and pliable dough. Turn on to a lightly floured board and knead. Wrap and chill in the refrigerator for 30 minutes.

4. Roll the pastry out on to a lightly floured surface or pastry board and use to line the oiled flan tin. Place in the refrigerator to reserve.

5. Warm the milk in a small saucepan. Briskly whisk together the eggs, egg yolk and caster sugar.

6. Pour the milk into the egg mixture and whisk until blended.

7. Strain through a sieve into the pastry case. Place the flan tin on a baking sheet.

8. Sprinkle the top of the tart with nutmeg and bake in the preheated oven for about 15 minutes.

9. Turn the oven down to 170°C/ 325°F/Gas Mark 3 and bake for a further 30 minutes, or until the custard has set. Serve hot or cold.

2

6

7

Caramelised Chocolate Tartlets

INGREDIENTS

Serves 6

350 g/12 oz ready-made shortcrust
  pastry, thawed if frozen
150 ml/¼ pint coconut milk
40 g/1½ oz demerara sugar
50 g/2 oz plain dark
  chocolate, melted
1 medium egg, beaten
few drops vanilla essence
1 small mango, peeled, stoned
  and sliced
1 small papaya, peeled, deseeded
  and chopped
1 star fruit, sliced
1 kiwi, peeled and sliced, or use fruits
  of your choice

1 Preheat the oven to 200°C/400°F/Gas Mark 6, 15 minutes before baking. Lightly oil 6 individual tartlet tins. Roll out the ready-made pastry on a lightly floured surface and use to line the oiled tins. Prick the bases and sides with a fork and line with nonstick baking parchment and baking beans. Bake blind for 10 minutes in the preheated oven, then remove from the oven and discard the baking beans and the baking parchment.

2 Reduce the oven temperature to 180°C/350°F/Gas Mark 4. Heat the coconut milk and 15 g/½ oz of the sugar in a heavy-based saucepan, stirring constantly until the sugar has dissolved. Remove the saucepan from the heat and leave to cool.

3 Stir the melted chocolate, the beaten egg and the vanilla essence into the cooled coconut milk. Stir until well mixed, then strain into the cooked pastry cases. Place on a baking sheet and bake in the oven for 25 minutes or until set. Remove and leave to cool, then chill in the refrigerator.

4 Preheat the grill, then arrange the fruits in a decorative pattern on the top of each tartlet. Sprinkle with the remaining demerara sugar and place the tartlets in the grill pan. Grill for 2 minutes or until the sugar bubbles and browns. Turn the tartlets, if necessary and take care not to burn the sugar. Remove from the grill and leave to cool before serving.

HELPFUL HINT

Before grilling, you may find it useful to cover the edges of the pastry with tinfoil to prevent it burning under the hot grill.

1

3

4

Chocolate Fruit Tiramisu

INGREDIENTS

Serves 4

2 ripe passion fruit

2 fresh nectarines or peaches

75 g/3 oz sponge finger biscuits

125 g/4 oz amaretti biscuits

5 tbsp amaretti liqueur

6 tbsp prepared black coffee

250 g/9 oz mascarpone cheese

450 ml/³/₄ pint fresh custard

200 g/7 oz plain dark chocolate,
    finely chopped or grated

2 tbsp cocoa powder, sifted

FOOD FACT

Mascarpone cheese is an Italian full fat cream cheese with a very thick, creamy texture and flavour. It is a classic ingredient of tiramisu. Here, it is mixed with some ready-made custard, which gives it a lighter texture.

1. Cut the passion fruit and scoop out the seeds and reserve. Plunge the nectarines or peaches into boiling water and leave for 2–3 minutes. Carefully remove the nectarines from the water, cut in half and remove the stones. Peel off the skin, chop the flesh finely and reserve.

2. Break the sponge finger biscuits and amaretti biscuits in half. Place the amaretti liqueur and prepared black coffee into a shallow dish and stir well. Place half the sponge fingers and amaretti biscuits into the amaretti and coffee mixture and soak for 30 seconds.

3. Lift out both biscuits from the liquor and arrange in the bases of 4 deep individual glass dishes.

4. Cream the mascarpone cheese until soft and creamy, then slowly beat in the fresh custard and mix well together.

5. Spoon half the mascarpone mixture over the biscuits in the dishes and sprinkle with 125 g/4 oz of the finely chopped or grated dark chocolate.

6. Arrange half the passion fruit seeds and the chopped nectarine or peaches over the chocolate and sprinkle with half the cocoa powder.

7. Place the remaining biscuits in the remaining coffee liqueur mixture and soak for 30 seconds, then arrange on top of the fruit and cocoa powder. Top with the remaining chopped or grated chocolate, nectarine or peach and the mascarpone cheese mixture, piling the mascarpone high in the dishes.

8. Chill in the refrigerator for 1¹/₂ hours, then spoon the remaining passion fruit seeds and cocoa powder over the desserts. Chill in the refrigerator for 30 minutes and serve.

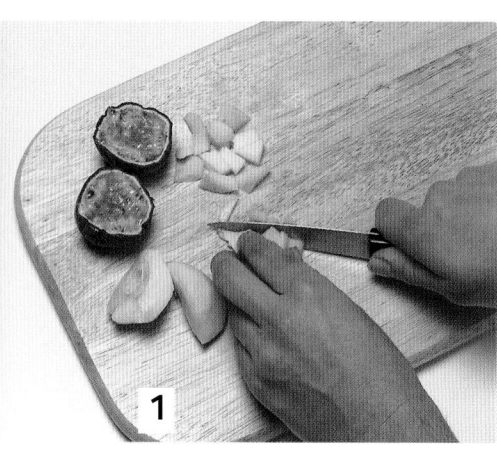

1

3

5

Crème Brûlée with Sugared Raspberries

INGREDIENTS

Serves 6

600 ml/1 pint fresh
  whipping cream
4 medium egg yolks
75 g/3 oz caster sugar
$\frac{1}{2}$ tsp vanilla essence
25 g/1 oz demerara sugar
175 g/6 oz fresh raspberries

HELPFUL HINT

Most chefs use blow torches to brown the sugar in step 7, as this is the quickest way to caramelise the top of the dessert. Take great care if using a blow torch, especially when lighting. Otherwise use the grill, making sure that it is very hot and the dessert is thoroughly chilled before caramelising the sugar topping. This will prevent the custard underneath from melting.

1 Preheat the oven to 150°C/300°F/Gas Mark 2. Pour the cream into a bowl and place over a saucepan of gently simmering water. Heat gently but do not allow to boil.

2 Meanwhile, whisk together the egg yolks, 50 g/2 oz of the caster sugar and the vanilla essence. When the cream is warm, pour it over the egg mixture briskly whisking until it is mixed completely.

3 Pour into 6 individual ramekin dishes and place in a roasting tin.

4 Fill the tin with sufficient water to come halfway up the sides of the dishes.

5 Bake in the preheated oven for about 1 hour, or until the puddings are set. (To test if set, carefully insert a round bladed knife into the centre, if the knife comes out clean they are set.)

6 Remove the puddings from the roasting tin and allow to cool. Chill in the refrigerator, preferably overnight.

7 Sprinkle the sugar over the top of each dish and place the puddings under a preheated hot grill.

8 When the sugar has caramelised and turned deep brown, remove from the heat and cool. Chill the puddings in the refrigerator for 2–3 hours before serving.

9 Toss the raspberries in the remaining caster sugar and sprinkle over the top of each dish. Serve with a little extra cream if liked.

2

5

7

Chocolate Profiteroles

INGREDIENTS

Serves 4

For the pastry:
150 ml/¼ pint water
50 g/2 oz butter
65 g/2½ oz plain flour, sifted
2 medium eggs, lightly beaten

For the custard:
300 ml/½ pint milk
pinch of freshly grated nutmeg
3 medium egg yolks
50 g/2 oz caster sugar
2 tbsp plain flour, sifted
2 tbsp cornflour, sifted

For the sauce:
175 g/6 oz soft brown sugar
150 ml/¼ pint boiling water
1 tsp instant coffee
1 tbsp cocoa powder
1 tbsp brandy
75 g/3 oz butter
1 tbsp golden syrup

1 Preheat the oven to 220°C/425°F/Gas Mark 7, 15 minutes before cooking. Lightly oil 2 baking sheets. For the pastry, place the water and the butter in a heavy-based saucepan and bring to the boil. Remove from the heat and beat in the flour. Return to the heat and cook for 1 minute or until the mixture forms a ball in the centre of the saucepan.

2 Remove from the heat and leave to cool slightly, then gradually beat in the eggs a little at a time, beating well after each addition. Once all the eggs have been added, beat until the paste is smooth and glossy. Pipe or spoon 20 small balls onto the baking sheets, allowing plenty of room for expansion.

3 Bake in the preheated oven for 25 minutes or until well risen and golden brown. Reduce the oven temperature to 180°C/ 350°F/Gas Mark 4. Make a hole in each ball and continue to bake for a further 5 minutes. Remove from the oven and leave to cool.

4 For the custard, place the milk and nutmeg in a heavy-based saucepan and bring to the boil. In another saucepan, whisk together the egg yolks, sugar and the flours, then beat in the hot milk. Bring to the boil and simmer, whisking constantly for 2 minutes. Cover and leave to cool.

5 Spoon the custard into the profiteroles and arrange on a large serving dish. Place all the sauce ingredients in a small saucepan and bring to the boil, then simmer for 10 minutes. Remove from the heat and cool slightly before serving with the chocolate profiteroles.

1

2

5

White Chocolate Eclairs

INGREDIENTS

Serves 4–6

50 g/2 oz unsalted butter
60 g/2½ oz plain flour, sifted
2 medium eggs, lightly beaten
6 ripe passion fruit
300 ml/½ pint double cream
3 tbsp kirsch
1 tbsp icing sugar
125 g/4 oz white chocolate, broken
  into pieces

HELPFUL HINT

Passion fruit are readily available in supermarkets. They are small, round purplish fruits that should have quite wrinkled skins. Smooth passion fruit are not ripe and will have little juice or flavour.

1 Preheat the oven to 190°C/375°F/Gas Mark 5, 10 minutes before baking. Lightly oil a baking sheet. Place the butter and 150 ml/¼ pint of water in a saucepan and heat until the butter has melted, then bring to the boil.

2 Remove the saucepan from the heat and immediately add the flour all at once, beating with a wooden spoon until the mixture forms a ball in the centre of the saucepan. Leave to cool for 3 minutes.

3 Add the eggs a little at a time, beating well after each addition until the paste is smooth, shiny and of a piping consistency. Spoon the mixture into a piping bag fitted with a plain nozzle. Sprinkle the oiled baking sheet with water. Pipe the mixture onto the baking sheet in 7.5 cm/3 inch lengths, using a knife to cut each pastry length neatly.

4 Bake in the preheated oven for 18–20 minutes, or until well risen and golden. Make a slit along the side of each eclair, to let the steam escape. Return the eclairs to the oven for a further 2 minutes to dry out. Transfer to a wire rack and leave to cool.

5 Halve the passion fruit, and using a small spoon, scoop the pulp of 4 of the fruits into a bowl. Add the cream, kirsch and icing sugar and whip until the cream holds it shape. Carefully spoon or pipe into the eclairs.

6 Melt the chocolate in a small heatproof bowl set over a saucepan of simmering water and stir until smooth.

7 Leave the chocolate to cool slightly, then spread over the top of the eclairs. Scoop the seeds and pulp out of the remaining passion fruit. Sieve. Use the juice to drizzle around the eclairs when serving.

2

4

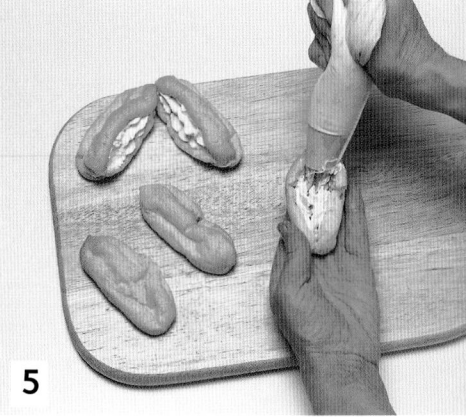

5

Pear & Chocolate Custard Tart

INGREDIENTS

Cuts into 6–8 slices

For the chocolate pastry:

125 g/4 oz unsalted butter, softened

60 g/2½ oz caster sugar

2 tsp vanilla essence

175 g/6 oz plain flour, sifted

40 g/1½ oz cocoa powder

whipped cream, to serve

For the filling:

125 g/4 oz plain dark
  chocolate, chopped

225 ml/8 fl oz whipping cream

50 g/2 oz caster sugar

1 large egg

1 large egg yolk

1 tbsp crème de cacao

3 ripe pears

HELPFUL HINT

The chocolate pastry is very soft so rolling it between sheets of cling film will make it much easier to handle without having to add a lot of extra flour.

1 Preheat the oven to 190°C/375°F/Gas Mark 5, 10 minutes before baking. To make the pastry, put the butter, sugar and vanilla essence into a food processor and blend until creamy. Add the flour and cocoa powder and process until a soft dough forms. Remove the dough, wrap in clingfilm and chill in the refrigerator for at least 1 hour.

2 Roll out the dough between 2 sheets of clingfilm to a 28 cm/11 inch round. Peel off the top sheet of clingfilm and invert the pastry round into a lightly oiled 23 cm/9 inch loose-based flan tin, easing the dough into the base and sides. Prick the base with a fork, then chill in the refrigerator for 1 hour.

3 Place a sheet of nonstick baking paper and baking beans in the case and bake blind in the preheated oven for 10 minutes. Remove the paper and beans and bake for a further 5 minutes. Remove and cool.

4 To make the filling, heat the chocolate, cream and half the sugar in a medium saucepan over a low heat, stirring until melted andsmooth. Remove from the heat and cool slightly before beating in the egg, egg yolk and crème de cacao. Spread evenly over the pastry case base.

5 Peel the pears, then cut each pear in half and carefully remove the core. Cut each half crossways into thin slices and arrange over the custard, gently fanning the slices towards the centre and pressing into the chocolate custard. Bake in the oven for 10 minutes.

6 Reduce the oven temperature to 180°C/350°F/Gas Mark 4 and sprinkle the surface evenly with the remaining sugar. Bake in the oven for 20–25 minutes, or until the custard is set and the pears are tender and glazed. Remove from the oven and leave to cool slightly. Cut into slices, then serve with spoonfuls of whipped cream.

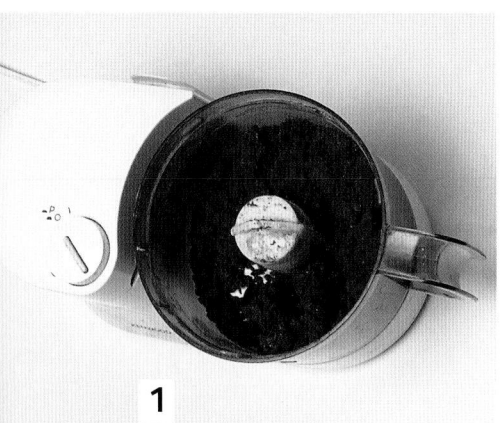

1

2

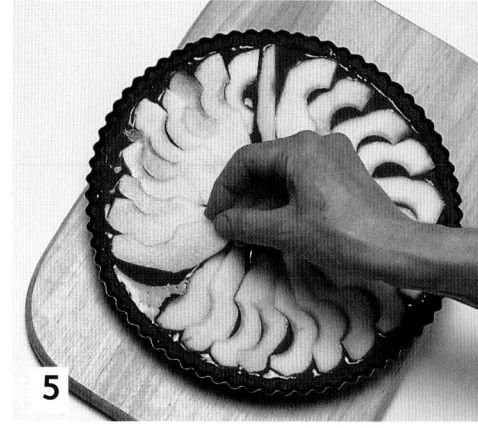

5

Hazelnut Meringues with Chocolate Sauce

INGREDIENTS

Serves 6

4 medium egg whites
225 g/8 oz caster sugar
125 g/4 oz ground hazelnuts
50 g/2 oz toasted hazelnuts, sliced
fresh berries, such as raspberries,
 strawberries and blueberries,
 to serve

For the chocolate sauce:

225 g/8 oz plain dark chocolate,
 broken into pieces
50 g/2 oz butter
300 ml/½ pint double cream
1 tbsp golden syrup

1 Preheat the oven to 150°C/300°F/Gas Mark 2, 10 minutes before baking. Line 2 baking sheets with nonstick baking parchment. Whisk the egg whites in a large grease-free bowl until stiff, then add the caster sugar, 1 teaspoonful at a time, whisking well after each addition. Continue to whisk until the mixture is stiff and dry, then using a metal spoon, fold in the ground hazelnuts.

2 Using 2 dessertspoons, spoon the mixture into 12 quenelle shapes onto the baking parchment. Sprinkle over the ground hazelnuts and bake in the preheated oven for 1½–2 hours or until dry and crisp. Switch the oven off and leave to cool in the oven.

3 To make the chocolate sauce, place the chocolate with the butter and 4 tablespoons of the cream and the golden syrup in a heavy-based saucepan and heat, stirring occasionally, until the chocolate has melted and the mixture is blended. Do not boil. Whip the remaining cream until soft peaks form.

4 Sandwich the meringues together with the whipped cream and place on serving plates. Spoon over the sauce and serve with a fresh berries.

HELPFUL HINT

It is important to add the sugar gradually when making meringues because if the sugar is not fully dissolved into the egg white it might leach out during cooking, making the meringues 'sweat'.

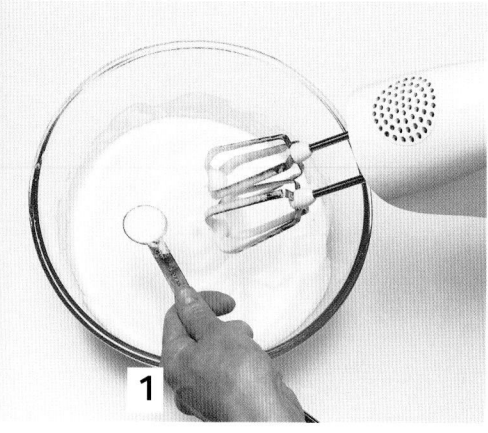
1

2

3

Mini Pistachio & Chocolate Strudels

INGREDIENTS

Makes 24

5 large sheets filo pastry
50 g/2 oz butter, melted
1–2 tbsp caster sugar for sprinkling
50 g/2 oz white chocolate, melted,
  to decorate

For the filling:

125 g/4 oz unsalted pistachios,
  finely chopped
3 tbsp caster sugar
50 g/2 oz plain dark chocolate,
  finely chopped
1–2 tsp rosewater
1 tbsp icing sugar for dusting

1 Preheat the oven to 170°C/325°F/Gas Mark 3, 10 minutes before baking. Lightly oil 2 large baking sheets. For the filling, mix the finely chopped pistachio nuts, the sugar and dark chocolate in a bowl. Sprinkle with the rosewater and stir lightly together and reserve.

2 Cut each filo pastry sheet into 4 to make 23 x 18 cm/9 x 7 inch rectangles. Place 1 rectangle on the work surface and brush with a little melted butter. Place another rectangle on top and brush with a little more butter. Sprinkle with a little caster sugar and spread about 1 dessertspoon of the filling along one short end. Fold the short end over the filling, then fold in the long edges and roll up. Place on the baking sheet seam-side down. Continue with the remaining pastry sheets and filling until both are used.

3 Brush each strudel with the remaining melted butter and sprinkle with a little caster sugar. Bake in the preheated oven for 20 minutes, or until golden brown and the pastry is crisp.

4 Remove from the oven and leave on the baking sheet for 2 minutes, then transfer to a wire rack. Dust with icing sugar. Place the melted white chocolate in a small piping bag fitted with a plain writing pipe and pipe squiggles over the strudel. Leave to set before serving.

TASTY TIP

Keep the unused filo pastry covered with a clean damp tea towel to prevent it from drying out.

1

2

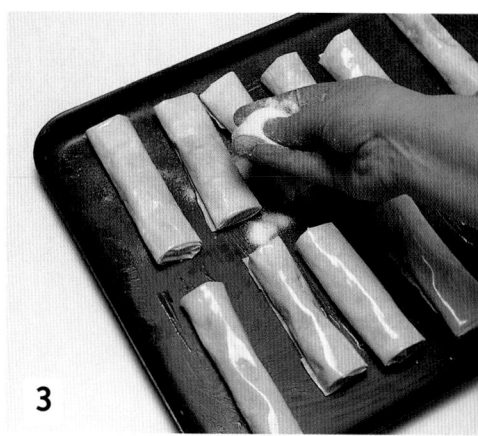

3

'Mars' Bar Mousse in Filo Cups

INGREDIENTS

Serves 6

6 large sheets filo pastry, thawed
if frozen
40 g/1½ oz unsalted butter, melted
1 tbsp caster sugar
3 x 60 g/2½ oz 'Mars' bars,
coarsely chopped
1½ tbsp milk
300 ml/½ pint double cream
1 large egg white
1 tsp cocoa powder
1 tbsp plain dark grated chocolate
chocolate sauce (see page 38), to
serve (optional)

For the topping:

300 ml/½ pint whipping cream
125 g/4 oz white chocolate, grated
1 tsp vanilla essence

TASTY TIP

When working with filo pastry, keep the dough that you are not using wrapped so it does not dry out.

1　Preheat the oven to 180°C/ 350°F/Gas Mark 4, 10 minutes before baking. Lightly oil 6 x 150 ml/¼ pint ramekins. Cut the filo pastry into 15 cm/6 inch squares, place 1 square on the work surface, then brush with a little of the melted butter, sprinkle with a little caster sugar. Butter a second square and lay it over the first at an angle, sprinkle with a little more caster sugar and repeat with 2 more pastry squares.

2　Press the assembled filo pastry into the oiled ramekin, pressing into the base to make a flat bottom and keeping the edges pointing up. Continue making the cups in this way, then place on a baking sheet and bake in the preheated oven for 10–15 minutes or until crisp and golden. Remove and leave to cool before removing the filo cups from the ramekins. Leave until cold.

3　Melt the 'Mars' bars and milk in a small saucepan, stirring constantly until melted and smooth. Leave to cool for 10 minutes, stirring occasionally.

4　Whisk the cream until thick and stir a spoonful into the melted 'Mars' bar mixture, then fold in the remaining cream. Whisk the egg white until stiff and fold into the 'Mars' bar mixture together with the cocoa powder. Chill the mousse in the refrigerator for 2–3 hours.

5　For the topping, boil 125 ml/4 fl oz of the whipping cream, add the grated white chocolate and vanilla essence and stir until smooth, then strain into a bowl and leave to cool. Whisk the remaining cream until thick, then fold into the white chocolate cream mixture.

6　Spoon the mousse into the filo cups, cover with the cream mixture and sprinkle with grated chocolate. Chill in the refrigerator before serving with chocolate sauce, if liked.

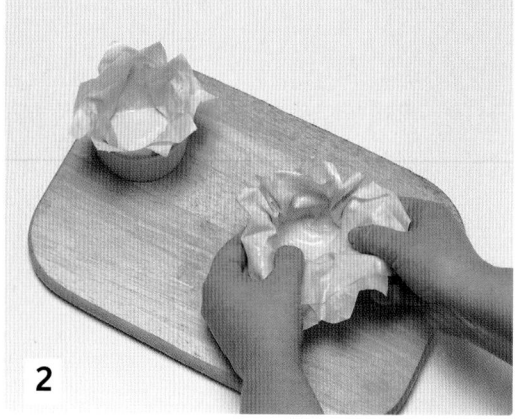

Chocolaty Puffs

INGREDIENTS

Makes 12 large puffs

For the choux pastry:
150 g/5 oz plain flour
2 tbsp cocoa powder
½ tsp salt
1 tbsp sugar
125 g/4 oz butter, cut into pieces
5 large eggs

For the chocolate cream filling:
225 g/8 oz plain dark
  chocolate, chopped
600 ml/1 pint double cream
1 tbsp caster sugar (optional)
2 tbsp crème de cacao (optional)

For the chocolate sauce:
225 g/8 oz plain dark chocolate
300 ml/½ pint whipping cream
50 g/2 oz butter, diced
1–2 tbsp golden syrup
1 tsp vanilla essence

1 Preheat the oven to 220°C/425°F/Gas Mark 7, 15 minutes before baking. Lightly oil a large baking sheet. To make the choux pastry, sift the flour and cocoa powder together. Place 250 ml/9 fl oz of water, the salt, sugar and butter in a saucepan and bring to the boil. Remove from the heat and add the flour mixture all at once, beating vigorously with a wooden spoon until the mixture forms a ball in the centre of the saucepan. Return to the heat and cook for 1 minute stirring, then cool slightly.

2 Using an electric mixer, beat in 4 of the eggs, 1 at a time, beating well after each addition. Beat the last egg and add a little at a time until the dough is thick and shiny and just falls from a spoon when tapped lightly on the side of the saucepan.

3 Pipe or spoon 12 large puffs onto the prepared baking sheet, leaving space between them. Cook in the preheated oven for 30–35 minutes, or until puffy and golden. Remove from the oven, slice off the top third of each bun and return to the oven for 5 minutes to dry out. Remove and leave to cool.

4 For the filling, heat the chocolate with 125 ml/4 fl oz of the double cream and 1 tablespoon of caster sugar, if using, stirring until smooth, then leave to cool. Whisk the remaining cream until soft peaks form and stir in the crème de cacao, if using. Quickly fold the cream into the chocolate, then spoon or pipe into the choux buns and place the lids on top.

5 Place all the ingredients for the sauce in a small saucepan and heat gently, stirring until smooth. Remove from the heat and leave to cool, stirring occasionally until thickened. Pour over the puffs and serve immediately.

1

3

5

Chocolate Pancakes

INGREDIENTS

Cuts into 8 slices

For the pancakes:
75 g/3 oz plain flour
1 tbsp cocoa powder
1 tsp caster sugar
¹/₂ tsp freshly grated nutmeg
2 medium eggs
175 ml/6 fl oz milk
75 g/3 oz unsalted butter, melted

For the mango sauce:
1 ripe mango, peeled and diced
50 ml/2 fl oz white wine
2 tbsp golden caster sugar
2 tbsp rum

For the filling:
225 g/8 oz plain dark chocolate
75 ml/3 fl oz double cream
3 eggs, separated
25 g/1 oz golden caster sugar

1 Preheat the oven to 200°C/400°F/Gas Mark 6, 15 minutes before cooking. To make the pancakes, sift the flour, cocoa powder, sugar and nutmeg into a bowl and make a well in the centre. Beat the eggs and milk together, then gradually beat into the flour mixture to form a batter. Stir in 50 g/2 oz of the melted butter and leave to stand for 1 hour.

2 Heat an 18 cm/7 inch nonstick frying pan and brush with a little melted butter. Add about 3 tablespoons of the batter and swirl to cover the base of the pan. Cook over a medium heat for 1–2 minutes, flip over and cook for a further 40 seconds. Repeat with the remaining batter. Stack the pancakes interleaving with greaseproof paper.

3 To make the sauce, place the mango, white wine and sugar in a saucepan and bring to the boil over a medium heat, then simmer for 2–3 minutes, stirring constantly. When the mixture has thickened add the rum. Chill in the refrigerator.

4 For the filling, melt the chocolate and cream in a small heavy-based saucepan over a medium heat. Stir until smooth, then leave to cool. Beat the egg yolks with the caster sugar for 3–5 minutes, or until the mixture is pale and creamy, then beat in the chocolate mixture.

5 Beat the egg whites until stiff, then add a little to the chocolate mixture. Stir in the remainder. Spoon a little of the mixture onto a pancake. Fold in half, then fold in half again, forming a triangle. Repeat with the remaining pancakes.

6 Brush the pancakes with a little melted butter and bake in the preheated oven for 15–20 minutes or until the filling is set. Serve hot or cold with the mango sauce.

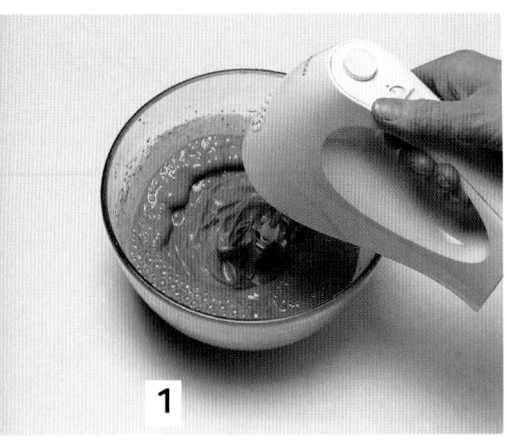
1

2

5

Apricot & Almond Slice

INGREDIENTS

Cuts into 10 slices

2 tbsp demerara sugar

25 g/1 oz flaked almonds

400 g can apricot
  halves, drained

225 g/8 oz butter

225 g/8 oz caster sugar

4 medium eggs

200 g/7 oz self-raising flour

25 g/1 oz ground almonds

½ tsp almond essence

50 g/2 oz ready-to-eat dried
  apricots, chopped

3 tbsp clear honey

3 tbsp roughly chopped
  almonds, toasted

1. Preheat the oven to 180°C/350°F/Gas Mark 4. Oil a 20.5 cm/8 inch square tin and line with non-stick baking paper.

2. Sprinkle the sugar and the flaked almonds over the paper, then arrange the apricot halves cut side down on top.

3. Cream the butter and sugar together in a large bowl until light and fluffy.

4. Gradually beat the eggs into the butter mixture, adding a spoonful of flour after each addition of egg.

5. When all the eggs have been added, stir in the remaining flour and ground almonds and mix thoroughly.

6. Add the almond essence and the apricots and stir well.

7. Spoon the mixture into the prepared tin, taking care not to dislodge the apricot halves. Bake in the preheated oven for 1 hour, or until golden and firm to touch.

8. Remove from the oven and allow to cool slightly for 15–20 minutes. Turn out carefully, discard the lining paper and transfer to a serving dish. Pour the honey over the top of the cake, sprinkle on the toasted almonds and serve.

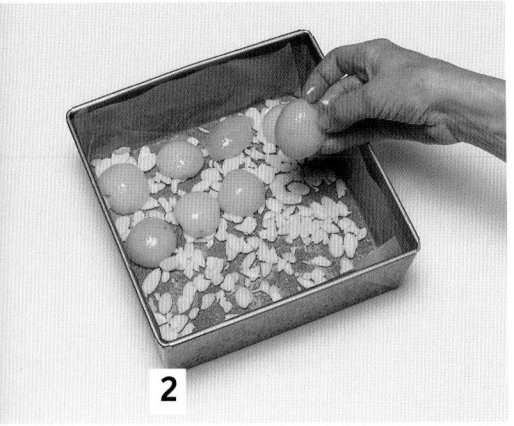

2

5

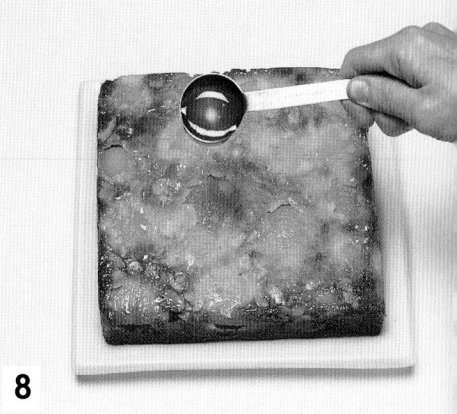

8

Baked Apple Dumplings

INGREDIENTS

Serves 4

225 g/8 oz self-raising flour
¼ tsp salt
125 g/4 oz shredded suet
4 medium cooking apples
4–6 tsp luxury mincemeat
1 medium egg white, beaten
2 tsp caster sugar
custard or vanilla sauce, to serve

TASTY TIP

To make vanilla sauce, blend 1½ tablespoons of cornflour with 3 tablespoons of milk to a smooth paste. Bring just under 300 ml/ ½ pint of milk to just below boiling point. Stir in the cornflour paste and cook over a gentle heat, stirring throughout until thickened and smooth. Remove from the heat and add 1 tablespoon of caster sugar, a knob of butter and ½ teaspoon of vanilla essence. Stir until the sugar and butter have melted, then serve.

1 Preheat the oven to 200°C/ 400°F/Gas Mark 6. Lightly oil a baking tray. Place the flour and salt in a bowl and stir in the suet.

2 Add just enough water to the mixture to mix to a soft but not sticky dough, using the fingertips.

3 Turn the dough on to a lightly floured board and knead lightly into a ball.

4 Divide the dough into 4 pieces and roll out each piece into a thin square, large enough to encase the apples.

5 Peel and core the apples and place 1 apple in the centre of each square of pastry.

6 Fill the centre of the apple with mincemeat, brush the edges of each pastry square with water and draw the corners up to meet over each apple.

7 Press the edges of the pastry firmly together and decorate with pastry leaves and shapes made from the extra pastry trimmings.

8 Place the apples on the prepared baking tray, brush with the egg white and sprinkle with the sugar.

9 Bake in the preheated oven for 30 minutes or until golden and the pastry and apples are cooked. Serve the dumplings hot with the custard or vanilla sauce.

2

6

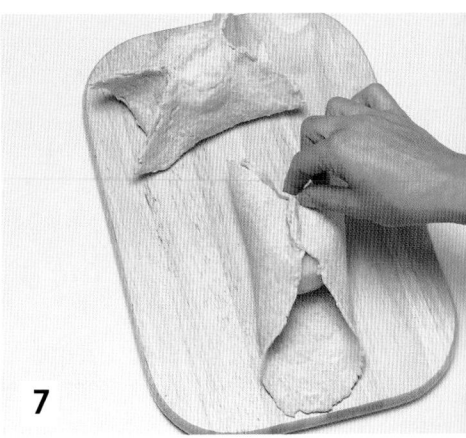
7

Jam Roly Poly

INGREDIENTS

Serves 6

225 g/8 oz self-raising flour
¼ tsp salt
125 g/4 oz shredded suet
about 150 ml/¼ pint water
3 tbsp strawberry jam
1 tbsp milk, to glaze
1 tsp caster sugar
ready-made jam sauce, to serve

TASTY TIP

To make jam sauce, warm 4 tablespoons of jam such as seedless raspberry jam with 150 ml/¼ pint of water or orange juice. Stir until smooth. Blend 2 teaspoons of arrowroot with 1 tablespoon of water or juice to a smooth paste. Bring the jam mixture to almost boiling point, then stir in the blended arrowroot. Cook, stirring until the mixture thickens slightly and clears, then serve.

1 Preheat the oven to 200°C/400°F/Gas Mark 6. Make the pastry by sifting the flour and salt into a large bowl.

2 Add the suet and mix lightly, then add the water a little at a time and mix to form a soft and pliable dough. (Take care not to make the dough too wet.)

3 Turn the dough out on to a lightly floured board and knead gently until smooth.

4 Roll the dough out into a 23 cm/9 inch x 28 cm/11 inch rectangle.

5 Spread the jam over the pastry leaving a border of 1 cm/½ inch all round. Fold the border over the jam and brush the edges with water.

6 Lightly roll the rectangle up from one of the short sides, seal the top edge and press the ends together. (Do not roll the pudding up too tightly.)

7 Turn the pudding upside down on to a large piece of greaseproof paper large enough to come halfway up the sides. (If using non-stick paper, then oil lightly.)

8 Tie the ends of the paper, to make a boat-shaped paper case for the pudding to sit in and to leave plenty of room for the roly poly to expand.

9 Brush the pudding lightly with milk and sprinkle with the sugar. Bake in the preheated oven for 30–40 minutes, or until well risen and golden. Serve immediately with the jam sauce.

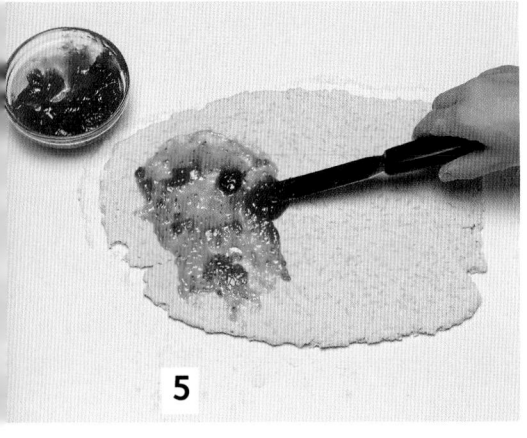

5

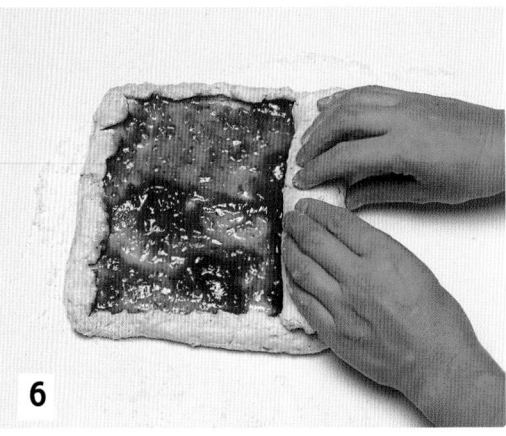

6

8

Step-by-Step, Practical Recipes Sweet Treats: Tips & Hints

Helpful Hint

Choux pastry, which is used in several recipes in this book, originated in France during the sixteenth century. Interestingly, choux pastry contains no raising agent, so the rise achieved during cooking relies upon the steam that is released as a consequence of the mixture's high moisture content. Although many find cooking a recipe with choux pastry an intimidating prospect, it is actually fairly simple; just make sure the oven is completely up to temperature before you put it in, and that the pastry is completely cooked before you remove it again.

Helpful Hint

Pastry needs to be kept as cool as possible throughout, so it is helpful to have cool hands and any liquids added to the mixture should be cold rather than allowed to reach room temperature. Also, make sure that the fat you add is not runny but firm, and avoid using too much flour when rolling out the pastry, as this can alter the proportions. Once the dough is prepared, roll it out in one direction and then allow it to rest for a while. When you come to line a flan case take care to choose the right tin; loose-bottomed metal flan cases tend to conduct heat more efficiently and evenly than ceramic dishes. Using a rolling pin, roll the pastry out until it is a few inches larger than the flan case and then carefully wrap the pastry around the rolling pin, lift and place into the tin. Carefully ease the pastry into the base and sides of the tin, allow to rest for a few minutes and then trim any excess pastry from the edges using a sharp knife.

Tasty Tip

Different desserts may be better suited to different seasons. This book contains great recipes for both hot and cold weather. For a chilly winter's evening, a pudding like Jam Roly Poly (page 46) or Baked Apple Dumplings (page 44) will be sure to warm you up. In the summer, when seasonal fruits such as strawberries are at their best, opt for a refreshing White Chocolate Mousse & Strawberry Tart (page 14).

Helpful Hint

When whisking egg whites for meringue, it is essential that the bowl being used is completely clean and dry, as any grease or oil will prevent the egg whites from gaining the necessary volume.

Tasty Tip

Decorate your sweet treats with handmade chocolate curls. Simply melt squares of chocolate in a glass bowl over hot water. Once melted, pour onto a cool surface, preferably marble, and leave until just set but not hard. You can then use a large cook's knife or cheese parer to form curls by pushing the blade across the surface of the chocolate at an angle.

Helpful Hint

Nuts are a useful ingredient to have to hand and are featured in many of the recipes in this book. To prevent them from spoiling between uses, why not try storing nuts in the freezer? Stored this way, whole nuts will keep for three years, shelled nuts for one year and ground nuts, such as ground almonds, for three months. Whole nuts will also crack far more easily when frozen, as their shells are much more brittle.

Food Fact

Sugar is a form of carbohydrate which is found only in foods originating from plants, such as fruits and sugarcane. Interestingly, sugar is actually an addictive substance as it activates the brain's reward system, which causes us to want more; no wonder we like sweet treats so much! In fact, suddenly removing refined sugar from your diet can even cause withdrawal symptoms such as tiredness and headaches.

Tasty Tip

Fruit is a delicious and colourful accompaniment to desserts and puddings. Try serving recipes containing dark or white chocolate with refreshing berries such as raspberries and strawberries, which will really complement the flavours. For sweeter desserts such as Lattice Treacle Tart (page 4) or those which already contain fruit such as Apricot and Almond Slice (page 42), why not serve warm with a dollop of cool Greek or natural yoghurt, which will not only cut down on the sweetness but will also provide an enjoyable contrast in temperature.

First published in 2013 by
FLAME TREE PUBLISHING LTD
Crabtree Hall, Crabtree Lane, Fulham,
London, SW6 6TY, United Kingdom
www.flametreepublishing.com

 The CIP record for this book is available from the British Library • Printed in China

NOTE: Recipes using uncooked eggs should be avoided by infants, the elderly, pregnant women and anyone suffering from an illness.

18 17 16 15 14 13   10 9 8 7 6 5 4 3 2 1

ISBN: 978-0-85775-855-2

ACKNOWLEDGEMENTS: Authors: Catherine Atkinson, Juliet Barker, Gina Steer, Vicki Smallwood, Carol Tennant, Mari Mererid Williams, Elizabeth Wolf-Cohen and Simone Wright. Photography: Colin Bowling, Paul Forrester and Stephen Brayne. Home Economists and Stylists: Jacqueline Bellefontaine, Mandy Phipps, Vicki Smallwood and Penny Stephens. All props supplied by Barbara Stewart at Surfaces. Publisher and Creative Director: Nick Wells. Editorial: Catherine Taylor, Laura Bulbeck, Esme Chapman and Emma Chafer. Design and Production: Chris Herbert, Mike Spender and Helen Wall.